A Most Urgent Task

Also by Derek Baines and published by Ginninderra Press
Flying Through Cloud

Derek Baines

A Most Urgent Task

Acknowledgements

'Alma Mater' first published in *Sun and Sleet*,
ed. John L. Sheppard, Poets Union, 2006

'Two People' first published in *Prismatics*,
ed. John L. Sheppard, Poets Union, 2008

For Margaret Baines

A Most Urgent Task
ISBN 978 1 74027 727 6
Copyright © text Derek Baines 2012
Cover image: Bradd Westmoreland, *Small Blue Portrait*, 2009, oil on
canvas, 20.5 x 25.5 cm; courtesy the artist and Gallery 9, Sydney

First published 2012
Reprinted 2016

GINNINDERRA PRESS
PO Box 3461 Port Adelaide SA 5015
www.ginninderrapress.com.au

Contents

Peeling a Mandarin	7
Unnamed, Unclaimed	9
Upping Anchor On the Future	10
Vodka Shots With Octogenarians	11
Alma Mater	12
Alma Mater II	13
Wild Dogs Scavenging	15
Roofs of Alexandria	16
Haiku	17
Sunday Night At Home	18
Night Vision	19
Two People	20
Memories of My Father	22
I Don't Know Who My Favourite Poet Is	23
Deadlines	24
High Altitude	25
Skin	27
Fisherman's Silence	28
Dromedary	30
Fire	31
Celebration	32
Popcorn	33
Picture Palace	34
Man at the Gym	36
Shower	37
After the City to Surf	38
Rest Stop	39
Tweezers	40
Ranking Among the World's Greatest Living Novelists	41
The Stack of Books On My Bedside Table	42

The Flattest Cat	45
Puddles	46
Passionfruit Vine on the Outhouse	47
Lollipop Rage	48
If It's Raining on the Day	49
Football Match Anxiety	50
Trampoline	51
Lunch Special at the Food Court in the Mall	52
Sitting On a Chair After Roughing It For a Week	53
Birds 1	54
Tilt Train To Howard	55
Puerto Vallarto Early Morning	56
Pines of Ritsurin Park	58
Navy	59
Jim Thompson Museum	60
Gold Coast From the Air	61
Haiku	62
Exit From the Metropolitan Museum of Art	63
Flying Through Cloud Again	64
At the Miyabayashi Inn	65
Waiting For People To Arrive	66
Ian Fairweather Lies Awake At Night	67
The Affair	68
Untitled	69
The Valley	70
Blank Canvas	71

Peeling a Mandarin

A mesh bag of mandarins,
sealed with a bow of string,
purchased from the fruit-seller
at the weekly produce market

In my right palm
I hold like a baseball the cool orange fruit
which will quench my thirst
or be a dry disappointment to over-ready senses.

I am right-handed but use my left thumb
to dig in,
stopping in time to prevent penetration
of the segments within
and a disastrous spillage of juice.

Perfect skin, unblemished like an infant's,
is not too thin as to be hard to peel,
not too thick as to shelter a desert inside.

The soft underside lodges under my thumbnail
making an indelible yellowed arc underneath

In my hand I hold a ball of juice
in a furry membrane,
nail pushes into the core

I prise off a segment.

Thumb and forefinger of the left hand,
still clutching the peel in its palm
bring the segment to my open lips.

Thirst and anticipation of perfection
bring teeth smashing down.

The bitter-sweet joy, uninterrupted by seed.

The bursting of the membrane,
squirting my mouth with juice.

Swallowing of pleasure.

Repeat nine times.

Unnamed, Unclaimed

Stigma of orphanhood –

a poem suffers as much
as a newborn child
abandoned on a garbage dump,
left to feral animals
to decide its fate.

The birth is the beginning
of the development
of personality and frame.

Until adulthood
it will rarely stand
on its feet without nurture
and guidance,
a roof over its head,
love,
and a name which suits.

Upping Anchor On the Future

A confluence of tide, sun and wind
of human dimension

A magnetic instant of clarity and peace

Fear is dispelled,
unbroken road ahead

It is completely up to me.

Accelerate.

Vodka Shots With Octogenarians

Stolichnaya neat
farewelling the departed
Happy times beckon
An ageless world possible
even as bodies grow old

Alma Mater

The campus,
savagely built in virgin bush,
expands year by year,
now politely,
but still without permission.

In the summer holiday
some students remain,
looking purposeful.
Are they conscientious
or unloved?

Dotting the bushland,
quiet as the snakes and insects,
the crouching ghosts of former students
hide from the riot police
during demonstrations over land rights,
uranium mining and civil liberties.

Buildings are named after men I knew
Are they dead, or merely revered?

We took more than we gave –
banked the knowledge,
fell in love,
smelt the wattle on spring evenings,
and heads resting
on inflated wine cask bladders,
drank in stars and cheap booze.

Alma Mater II

Great Hall of 1868,
choir in the sunlight
through the stained glass window,
filtering the figures of history
onto our faces
intent on the choirmaster's
hands,
(man of Oxbridge with a bad temper
although respected).

School had outgrown
the Great Hall already –
no more assembling there,
but weddings and funerals
and choir practice,
and the carved messages
of frustrated boys on the pews.

Now a famous poet
of Brisbane
comes to the school to read
from his work of
Typewriter Music,
the sweet voices of prepubescent
choirboys permeated
in the bricks.

One day, with Sir's permission,
we took apart the wooden steps
leading to the pulpit
to uncover the mystery below –
was it a foundation stone or a gravestone
we were looking for, I can't recall –
and shone inquiring lights
into the dark.
Much like Sir was trying to do
upon his blank boys in his day job
as an English teacher.

We found nothing under that pulpit,
from which the headmaster
and ministers and great poets
spoke to the future leaders,
fathers and lovers of their shaping,
their only authority words,
and the lectern on the wooden floor,
covering a dark space.

Accumulated dust of 140 years
of boys' education.

Wild Dogs Scavenging

The father wanders off
looking busy and responsible.

The mother
thinking of food for the family,
and playing with one pup,
lets another nip at her leg.

Father returns proud
and in charge,
but with nothing
to show for himself.

Mother nudges a pup
in the direction of some scraps
and sits in the dirt
to scratch her fleas,
a most urgent task.

Roofs of Alexandria

A new sash window
cut out of the side of the house
reveals three grey roofs
each of different tone
and with its own cut-out,
beckoning the sun to enter
and nourish the human contents.

Today the sky is the hue of the roofs.

On one
sits a Victorian chimney
like a clogged lung,
a now useless appendage
turned into itself
nursing the soot and tar within.

Inside this window is my new writing space.

Tomorrow if the sky is blue
the roofs might glisten
as the sea,
with corrugated iron ripples.

In the winter the chimney
might sputter and clear.
If I see a wisp of smoke
I will be witnessing
a medical miracle.

Haiku

What is the trigger
for the bud of the cherry
to break free this year?

Sunday Night At Home

With a plate of Mum's stew on toast,
a glass of wine,

the decision not to go out,

the realisation that the weekend
      is finite,

the knowledge that friends are
      one's beautiful strength and measure
but they want Sunday night
      at home too

Night Vision

Gum trees scratching
the full moon outside the window
as the train accelerates.

Two People

The light, warming us,
is carried in through the windowpanes
of each age of our marriage,
through the bevelled glass,

glass we clean in the old way,
once a month
with newspaper and methylated spirits

glass cracked in one corner
by the eucalypt branch
during a cyclone,
shaken and enraged in its wooden cage
by the wind.

Morning light, clear and straight
across the sea from the east
has been filtered in recent years
through a thick maturity of garden.

Then in the autumn
on our afternoon walk,
with the turning of the leaves,
we can see up the hill through the trees,
see through the window
our young selves moving about inside.

In the highest pane,
we are playing in the kitchen,
cookbook stained with greasy fingerprints
propped up on the bench,
offering a taste of an experimental sauce
on a new wooden spoon.

In the middle pane,
hanging a treasured new painting
on freshly-prepared white walls.
We debate its meaning.

And in the lowest pane,
exposure of niggling bad habits,
forgiven even in old age.

Now, at night, we often sit inside by the window,
clothed in the moonlight,
together making out the pattern
of the Southern Cross,
never thinking to draw the curtains against the sky.

Memories of My Father

When he arrived home
from work
we danced our strange dance
down the hallway
as I stood on his feet
and let him lead.
It was 1965.

Going to his office
on Saturday morning
and playing with the
typewriters and adding machines
then the greengrocer
and then the butcher.
No expectorating it said –
I thought it meant
looking around and
not buying anything
It was 1968.

Joyride
for my twelfth birthday
he flew the plane
1973.

I Don't Know Who My Favourite Poet Is

It's not something that has been forgotten.

I've never known it.

I doubt my right to have a favourite
When I am not sufficiently well-read.

One can sometimes get away with lying about it
but in the end what does it prove?

– only that you can successfully deceive
without blushing.

Deadlines

A tightrope walk
between inspiration and clarity
on one side

and the quicksand
of mediocrity
on the other.

Falling.

High Altitude

First of the group
to get above the crowd,
taking it in,
what's going on,
who's going where.

Straight up,
no gnarls
or embarrassing offshoots.

Dogs, out of respect,
come and sniff,
but dare not pee.

Time spent quietly listening,
watching,
moving toward the sun,
shaking in the cold rain
and wind.

An elegant soaring bird,
welcomed,
finds its high-altitude home.

Still growing, co-existing,
there's space for everyone
if you take it slow
and keep an eye
on the neighbours' subtle shifting

But as from the lighthouse
on Gabo Island,
we receive necessary
and irrefutable messages.

Sometimes if one is special,
like visiting a secret tree house,
or sitting on your friend's shoulders,
there's a chance
to share the singular view.

The colour and the light come naturally,
good words come from up there.

Skin

Papery dry skin
on the back of his hand,
so prominent a place
seen a hundred times a day

A slow subtle change
realised this day,
like a blow to the head
by an intruder broken in
through the roof.

Fisherman's Silence

His silence is his life
raging in its self.

There has never been
purer thought,
talk, laughter,
and appreciation of his lover
than in this silence.

I watch from the beach
his immovable back and arms
flick the rod to move the baited hook
or to show he is not
a statue.

Peeling Away

Digital/Analogue/Telephone/Newspaper
Conversation, face-to-face,
      with another unpeeled human
Full sentences, a hearty home-cooked meal
      of dialogue
Forgotten words, uncovered as if fossils
Questions I've meant to pose
Answers I've waited for
Thoughts, formulated in neat bundles
Opinions, presented and admired
Jokes, punchlines remembered
      and delivered with sharp timing
Laughter, loosening the body for friendship
Warmth, permeating from dry creek beds
Articulate serenity/Peace/A notebook/Poetry

Dromedary

The grand weight 'ushes' down
on calloused knees.

Her brother calls in protest
as the saddle is adjusted.
A serene blink of long-lashed eyes
is her only concession to discomfort.

Teeth of piano keys I dare not play
wrapped in full lips that might stretch
around a desert oak.
Plaited tail, belly fattened on sorghum.

Down her neck, a delicate scarf
of grey wool,
gifted by an admirer.

Fire

Centre of community,
of light and heat.
Respected like a graceful
wild animal.

Waru

Fire-walking in the silent coals,
mind pinpointing a place
of no pain.

Spark for a bushfire's cauldron
Demon of destruction
Giver of renewal.

Celebration

A celebration being had
just tucked up on the sofa
with the weekend papers
and your lover,
reading the news
and each other's minds,
dreams and thoughts
crossing the rainy day sky.

Then add old friends
(who know you too well
to let the milestone
go unmarked
or be relaxed away)
arriving to fill
the pure peaceful void
with laughter and wine.

Later, one of them
sits in the corner
scratching down a poem
to wrap and ribbon the occasion
and show it to you
in another light.

Popcorn

Birth in fertile fields, captured and sent
to a humid prison, smeared in oil
and transformed, popping,
into a snack for the entertained rich.
Devoured in a pre-dinner frenzy,
nourishment for a harrowing
        cinematic journey.
Lone clinging survivor in the folds
        of a sweater,
unseen in the flickering light of the movie.
Undiscovered until after the credits
        have rolled,
it falls on the floor into the relief
of the house lights.
No match for the usher's dustpan and brush,
twenty times bigger
than its vulnerable yet brave self.

Picture Palace

Courtship.

Unrequited longings of sad single cinema-goers.

Inexperienced fumblings of American servicemen
with young Brisbane
on Saturday nights during World War II.

Cheating couples in the back of the stalls.

My mother, me, school holidays in 1970,
a trip to town on the bus,
Julie Andrews in *Darling Lili*
(was that the one she bared her breasts in?)
followed by a green soda drink in David Jones' basement.

High school days protest
helped save the auditorium shell and
the grand foyer
from an overactive property developer.
Now we fight all over again.

Let's have a sherry in the bar before the session.

I hope there will be spare seats in the dress circle tonight.

Do you think the organist will play?
(Is there much room down there under the stage?)

Damn these shorts, when is the movie going to start?

Stifling the urge to scream out
at the open-mouthed popcorn muncher.
His rudeness gives me the right, though.

The flickering of the screen
and the reflected thoughts of the audience.
Memories have been pumped into this air,
absorbed by these walls, these seats, at the bar
and the candy counter.
The social record of the city, they are suspended in here.

Frank Thring Sr's stirred ghost
ruminates on how this history
will escape when the eighty-year-old roof is taken off.

Reg, that must've been one of the best fil-ums
I've ever seen.

A nightcap on the way out, my love?

Man at the Gym

Symmetry defies
His size attracts attention
Others not compelled to touch
steroid-killed beauty.
Mirrored face his only love

Shower

I reach for 'Cold'.
Twisting counter-clockwise
my hand meets no resistance.

I dive in
standing up.

I drink
not opening my mouth.

I feel the drought-breaking
rain on my skin.

After the City to Surf

Mad-eyed, shirtless muscle
still on an oxygen high,
levitating into the St James Station
pedestrian tunnel.

Rest Stop

The young man,
nostrils slammed by the stench,
trying not to wet his shoes,
is standing on the grid
next to a truck driver –
tall, beefy, or maybe close to fat –
hard to tell with a sideways glance
in the second he is allowed

Baggy jeans,
red-checked flannelette shirt,
running shoes.
Adjusting his stance,
feet about twelve inches apart,
the truckie pops open the buttons of his fly
with his left hand
and pulls his driving companion out
with the right,
lets it hang right down in front and
delivers a bucketful
of pseudo-ephedrine laced
piss

About 250 miles till I get home
to the wife, he tells himself,
rubbing insomniac's eyes
with his giant hands.

Tweezers

Front gardens a little overgrown
can be thought charming

Errant hairs
straying beyond the divide
spoil the face's landscape.

Ivy advancing its years
up the front brick wall
admired by the passer-by.

Hair clambering
up the top of the nose-bridge
reaching left and right
to complete the monobrow,
enemy of fashion.

Same hair that would be
lush growth on the head and admired
is declared a weed in the ears
and eradicated by the vigilant.

Whatever of yours grows
on the neighbour's side of the fence
is sight unseen –
the hairy back of the garden.

Tweezer,
gardening tool of the human landscape.

Ranking Among the World's Greatest Living Novelists

To be considered
as one of the world's
greatest living novelists
would be a fine sobriquet.

It means one is alive,
a truly refreshing,
exhilarating state,
and great.

Furthermore,
being one of the best,
not yet the best,
gives one a little goal
to aim for.

The alternative –
death and perfection?

The Stack of Books On My Bedside Table

(My literary peak)

I was testing my luck
to rest a glass of water
on the top
of an encyclopaedic mountain
of my own slow dozy making.

A few solid magazines
of significant dimension
lay a firm foundation.

A rather small climb
to the literary base station
with Joyce's *Ulysses*
solid as granite,
immovable and unopened
under sedimentary layers
of easier and more accessible material.

A trek up the steppes
of Zadie Smith *On Beauty*
still undiscovered under
the century's lava flow,
a solid mass trapping
Vernon God Little
frozen in its Booker-winning state.

The broken-spined paperback body
of *A Suitable Boy*.
He couldn't carry the weight
of the words.
And now fused together
under the pressure
of *History of Australia* Volume 5 then 4,
because I often like to read things back-to-front
to first see how they end.
But in this case the font is too small
for late at night.

A light leafy layer
of Augusten Burroughs *Running with Scissors*
would eventually be carbonised
if my mountain is stable
for thousands of years.

Perhaps it was *Austerlitz* that caused
the rumblings and instability on my peak –
the ideas of Sebald, his delicious tangents,
the unresolved story of Austerlitz's father,
the characters and the author talking
beyond the grave.

When this high-pressure steam was released,
the copy of last week's *Sydney Morning Herald Review*,
roughly folded in two,
had no chance whatsoever when the glass
of water was placed on top.

Tired red eyes not taking care
to aim for the midpoint
of the understructure,
my literary peak (such as it was),
hadn't lasted more than a few months.

Now with its geological fragments
strewn across my bedroom floor,
I had to start to rebuild –
this time more stable and considered,
for longevity.

The Flattest Cat

The epitome
of flat, already a stole:
some huge truck tyre,
flat cat.

Puddles

Puddle is not a manly word
especially when you step in one.

Passionfruit Vine on the Outhouse

Sitting any longer
on this toilet
will surely see the
tendrils of the passionfruit vine
creep through the crack
in the outhouse door
as they seek a stable place,

Cling to my neck
and make me part
of their world.

Will the fat spider
(now sleeping in its web) –
confidante, collaborator
of the vine
wake and salivate at the
immobile human feast,
bite me to a cardiac arrest,
then devour?

Lollipop Rage

I can only contain my rage
for another two minutes maximum
against the man
sitting opposite me
in the library reading room
eating a lollipop.
They are meant to be sucked.

He has finished now,
and I have run out of excuses
to not do my work.

Now he is crunching on the stick!

And his neighbour
is having a webcam conversation
on his laptop,
trying to be discreet.
It must be with a lover
as under the table
he is nervously crossing and uncrossing
his feet
one with a pink sock
and one with red.

If It's Raining on the Day

'We need a contingency plan,
should it be raining on the day.'

'It won't rain.'

'But it might rain,
as all reasonable people know.'

'Are you calling me unreasonable?'

'No, we merely need a contingency.'

So it is, the battle we keep
with risk
and the unknowns
of some future time

When every moment
changes history's course,
who can predict
if a picnic will be washed out?

And how much certainty
could we survive?

Football Match Anxiety

This Wednesday night
is the State of Origin

Ask my opinion

and you will sense anxiety
because I do not get it.

Trampoline

I fell from the window
eleven metres to the concrete pavement
whilst cleaning the windows.

Spirits rose and the fractures healed.

At the end I want
to be on the dance floor
wearing stilettos.

Lunch Special at the Food Court in the Mall

It does not closely
resemble the photograph
of enchiladas
illuminated
above the counter.

Sitting On a Chair After Roughing It For a Week

Balanced gluteus maximus,
left and right.
Thighs at ninety degrees to the torso
Back straight

An angle that is more comfortable
as I mature with each new moon

A swag or tree branch
being an acceptable bush substitute,
a chair, moulded for a man,
is perfection for my ass,
cupping it in a firm grip.

Birds 1

My poetry teacher
said just go
to the park
and write
about birds.

I've sweated here for an hour
There is not a bird to be seen
and I doubt KL
will believe it.

Perhaps the day is too perfect
and they've all gone on a trip.

Tilt Train To Howard

Train arrives
Skinny boy in white singlet stretches
holding a fag
and his girlfriend jumps up
and sits on his hips facing him.

Overweight companion
looks awkward but loyal
wondering when his turn
will come
Baseball cap on sideways.

Puerto Vallarto Early Morning

Up the coast
a ten-story cruise ship
is slowly turned by tugs.
The sun drags itself
above the eastern mountains
to light it up

Two brothers maybe five years old
collect aluminium cans,
their father shadowing them
in his rattling pick-up truck.

Shrimps being barbecued
to be sold later on the beach
with lime juice and tabasco

A sun-dried beach kiosk operator
sifts and cleans his sand

Taxi drivers patiently return
drug-fucked partygoers to resorts
and wait at the rank for a fare

A line of men stand
on the concrete pier
with fishing lines in hand.
No fish, but plentiful camaraderie.

Joggers disturbing the sleepy natural order
which still holds my old friend prisoner
back at the hotel room,
unable to see the hidden business
of morning
but dreaming vividly
under his white cotton sheet.

Pines of Ritsurin Park

Clipped pines,
limbs wrapped and stretched
by twenty generations of gardeners
and four centuries of grotesquery.

Iron maidens
undefiable in their own territory,
a stare stops a newcomer dead.

Relaxing, then rearranging
their now haggard bodies
behind one's back.

Memories of watching in girlish excitement
as handsome nobles on horseback
challenged each other
in an archery competition.

Sheltering the Kigetsutei Teahouse
from the summer sun,
attracting compliments.

Ever loyal to the feudal lord Matsudaira,
now but ashes at their feet.

Navy

Two inexperienced young spies
on an 'academic research trip'
to a Japanese naval port
choose a hotel
at random

A modest
yet comfortable room
without bath

In the communal tub,
soaking of feet
and lazy staring out to sea.

In the near view
of the buildings next door,
a young man in his room
changing clothes.

But there are eight
beds in there!
Now another man
in the same clothes.

The naval dormitory.

A career-enhancing
fluke.

This is a luxury hotel.

Jim Thompson Museum

Purple, white lotus
tower in the pond of carp
Thai garden in spring.

Gold Coast From the Air

Concrete spikes,
foundations of some
larger-than-life construction
await the placement
of the real thing on top.

Airside view dwarfs the giants
of the ground made by men,
casting shadows
on children digging in the sand.

Now as we move south-west
it's replaced by green hinterland,
headwaters of rivers
and rejuvenation.

Haiku

Two Japanese girls
on the slow Wollongong train
I do get their point.

Exit From the Metropolitan Museum of Art

A decision to leave is bearable
only if you resolve to return one day.

A great freight train of questioning,
enlightenment, stimulation and beauty
carries you down the main stairs
a few feet above the granite,
polished by the generations of feet.

It slows through the great hall,
passing hundreds awaiting
the next departure,
mostly first-timers queuing
for an amusement park ride.

Five large urns of fresh lilies,
'The continuing gift of Lila Acheson Wallace',
are complimentary dessert
in a sensuous banquet.

The light at the end of the tunnel
is Fifth Avenue.

Flying Through Cloud Again

Turning my head for an instant's distraction,
the morning world
outside the little pressurised window
turns from a remarkable landscape
to an impenetrable grey wool.

The fog lifts,
and we are now flying high
across a valley of sea,
cloudy shifting islands
the stopping-off points
of a giant, lighter than air,
playing hopscotch.

Now there are furrowed fields
covered in mist.
Do the crops lay unharmed beneath?

At the Miyabayashi Inn

Gentle rain falls
on the roof of ten generations,
the pond fills.

The garden of Minshuku Miyabayashi
welcomes visitors.

Nothing has changed.

Waiting For People To Arrive

That is in fact what I am doing.

Doing the dishes on 'fast' cycle,
hiding things in cupboards,
abandoning the more intricately-
planned recipe ideas for store-bought.

Also writing a poem –
as they are literary people
      the ones coming over –
to get me
in the mood.

They are meeting here
to discuss
Gabriel Garcia Marquez's
Love in the Time of Cholera.

Does Gabo do book club?

Ian Fairweather Lies Awake At Night

Familiar scurrying of rats
across the beams
of the thatched roof;
goannas lie in wait.

In Bribie Island bushland,
Fairweather evokes
his days in the Far East
and sees an intricate
Chinese character,
its brush strokes
to be followed tomorrow
in oil on a fresh canvas.

In Sydney
a gallerist finalises the hang
of his latest record-breaking
Ian Fairweather show
by bright incandescent light,
while the crepuscular vision
of the artist himself,
remembered from hours earlier
when he lay down early
on his sleeping mat,
foments a new work.

Later, another is inspired
by the rays
filtered through fragrant eucalypts
and through his own eyes,
adjusting slowly to the morning.

The Affair

She is 'having an affair'.

This sounds a bit too casual,
she tells her best girlfriend,
like she is 'having an ice-cream'.

It's more like
she is 'creating an affair'
or 'causing an affair'.

She hopes that
she won't soon be
'recovering from an affair'
or rebuilding her life
'after an affair'.

Untitled

I don't want to hide it
but I don't want
to announce it either.

So I will leave it untitled
and enjoy it quietly by myself
at this point.

The Valley

Cicadas guard the spot
where the house will be

It's hard to see
the cicadas
as the house
is still a concept

Blank Canvas

Amnesia of his former society,
the prisoner released on parole
after thirty years in custody

Amnesia of the records and
photographs of his life –
a new beginning after the flood,
without insurance money

Amnesia drug administered
for a medical procedure
Doctor advises good news –
we didn't find anything.

Divorce,
move to a new city

Aron Ralston
cuts his own arm off

New beginnings, of necessity
All blank canvases

Masterpieces await.

www.ingramcontent.com/pod-product-compliance
Lightning Source LLC
Chambersburg PA
CBHW062154100526
44589CB00014B/1831